Gioachino
ROSSINI
L'ITALIANA IN ALGERI
SINFONIA

Edited by
Clark McAlister

Study Score
Partitur

SERENISSIMA MUSIC, INC.

PREFACE

To be as popular as they are, the overtures to Rossini's operas have been treated very poorly by publishers, both Italian and foreign, throughout most of their histories. Even the most recent editions, as thorough as many of them are, do not answer all of the questions concerning textual matters.

It will probably always be so. First, many of the textual inconsistencies one finds come from Rossini's own manuscripts. During most of his career, Rossini was working at an incredibly fast and furious pace, so it is not surprising that some relatively small details would escape his attention. Also, working at such speed inevitably took a toll on the legibility of some of his manuscripts, thereby adding another layer of potential uncertainty. While the context will frequently clarify such matters, in numerous cases different readings are possible.

Second, these scores come from a time when performance practices still assumed that the written score would be modified in performance in certain fairly predictable ways. Broadly speaking, for example, a certain lightness of execution was expected, the notation of which in our own era requires a rather liberal use of staccato dots. In Rossini's time, this refinement of notation was not practiced.

Third, in the case of works written for the stage which were already frequently performed during the composer's lifetime, it is quite logical to believe that Rossini's manuscript scores represent only an intermediate stage in the perfection of his music. The world of opera, more than that of concert music, thrives on revisions and alterations. Many of these changes, of course, are made to suit specific circumstances, and the composer would not want them to become permanent. Norman Del Mar, in his invaluable book *Orchestra Variations*, points out that, on the other hand, some of these changes represent composer-sanctioned second thoughts and even, sometimes, improvements over the original version of the text to be found in the manuscript score. As Del Mar says, "Not all traditions are bad and many derive from the composer himself or the society to which he belonged."

The question, then, becomes how to distinguish one kind of change from the other—when a later source differs from an earlier one, which reading should be followed? If we accept that in many instances no definitive answer is possible, we must follow our best understanding of Rossini's style, both as an individual composer and as one working contentedly within the prevailing performance practices of his time. The present editions of these overtures seek to do just that—by examining as many sources as possible, to arrive at performing texts which both reflect the spirit of the composer and are as practical as possible for the use of modern orchestras.

There is one aspect of this and other scores of Rossini's that needs more clarification than will fit practically in the space of a footnote. One of Rossini's favorite string colors is the rhythmic tapping, or clicking, of the bow against the string, indicated by the instruction **battute**, or "beaten." Some writers (including Christine Amner in *The A to Z of Foreign Musical Terms* and Walter Kolneder in *Auffürungspraxis bei Vivaldi*) feel that this instruction at least implies execution by using the wood of the bow, col legno. But Norman Del Mar, in *A Companion to the Orchestra*, suggests otherwise. In his discussion of the term col legno he writes:

> It is true that if executed honestly with only the wood of the bow very little actual note is heard, and when composers write important note formations col legno, such Berlioz in the Witches' Sabbath movement of *Symphonie fantastique*, the players will generally cheat by turning the bows sideways to that a little of the hair also comes into play. If they cheat too much, only the hair being brought into contact with the strings, this creates a quite different device, which is found constantly in Rossini under the term battute. . . . None of these vertical techniques produces any enormous volume, especially in view of the cautious attitude of the musicians . . .

To this discussion, three further considerations may be added. First, it will be seen that this technique also yields a staccato "sound," so that the use of staccato dots in notating its use is unnecessary. Second, there are passages which lend themselves to this style of playing but for which Rossini did not indicate battute. When, in these editions, the editor suggests the use of this technique the term [battute] will appear, but the composer's staccato indications will be retained. Finally, Rossini is sometimes not clear about when players should return from battute to conventional arco, whether staccato or not. Although the context may seem to make these changeover points evident, in these editions battute will always be "cancelled" by the term arco.

I wish to thank Nancy M. Bradburd of the Philadelphia Orchestra and Clinton F. Nieweg, Librarian (retired) of that Orchestra, for their insights and suggestions during the preparation of these editions. I am most fortunate to be able to partake of their vast experience in these matters.

The Editor
Spring 2014

ORCHESTRA

Piccolo

2 Oboes

2 Clarinets (C)

Bassoon

2 Horns (C)

2 Trumpets (C)

Timpani

Percussion

Violins I

Violins II

Violas

Violoncellos

Double Basses

Duration: ca. 7 minutes
Premiere: May 22, 1813
Venice
Teatro San Benedetto
Soli, Chorus and Orchestra / Alessandro Rolla

Edwin F. Kalmus, LC
P. O. Box 5011
Boca Raton, FL 33431-0811
Phone: 561-241-6340; 800-434-6340
Fax: 561-241-6347
Website: www.efkalmus.com

L'ITALIANA IN ALGERI
SINFONIA

Gioachino Rossini
Performing edition by Clark McAlister

SERENISSIMA MUSIC, INC.

* In some sources, the Double Basses do not play this measure.

* In some sources, the Double Basses do not play mm. 25-26.

4

* Oboe m. 27 and Clarinet m. 29: Several sources show this rhythm:

42097

* The sources aren't clear; in this measure and similar places, the indication could be either an accent > or a diminuendo ⎯>.

* This and similar figures to be played on the beat.

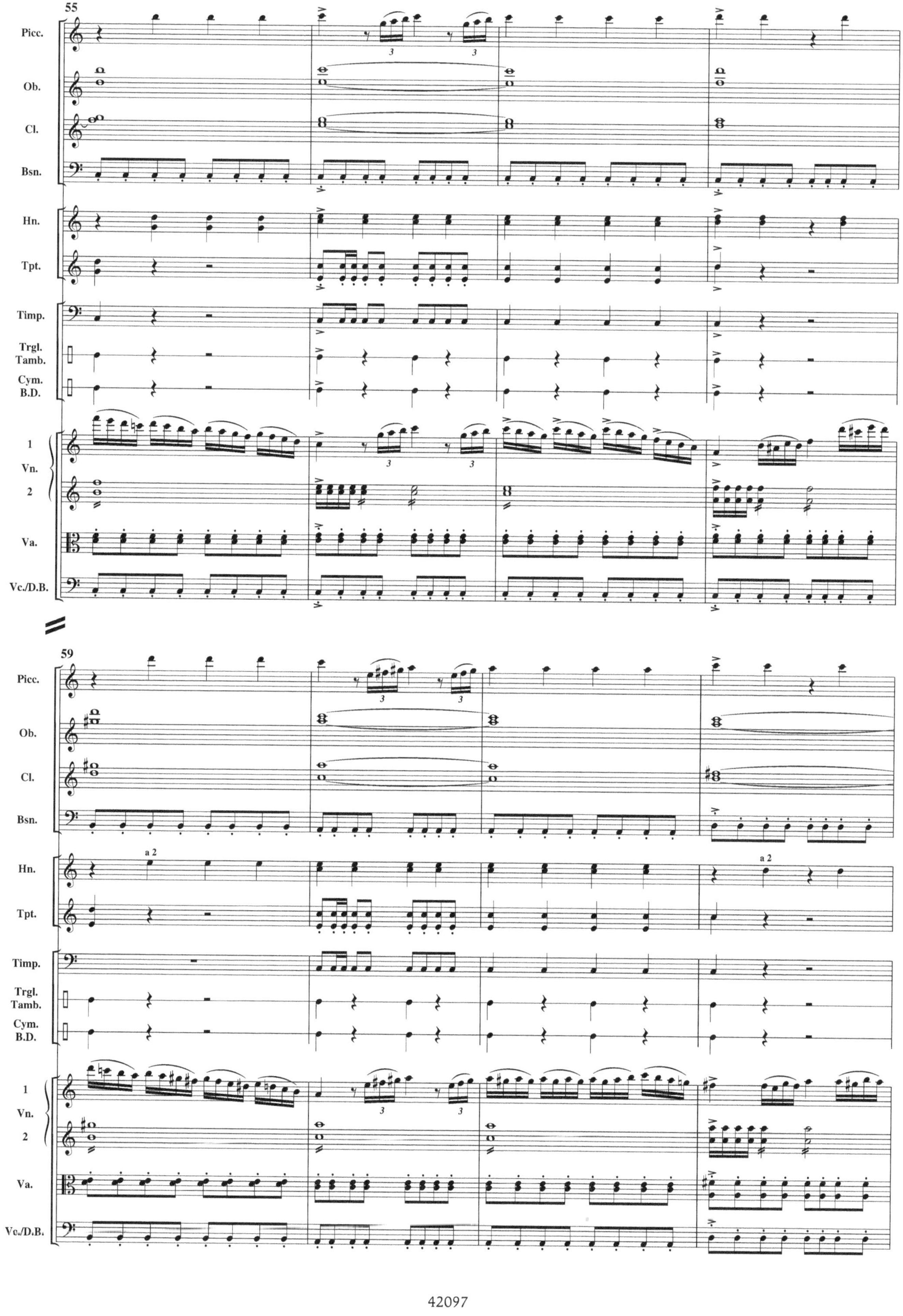
55
Picc.
Ob.
Cl.
Bsn.
Hn.
Tpt.
Timp.
Trgl.
Tamb.
Cym.
B.D.
1
Vn.
2
Va.
Vc./D.B.
59
a 2

63
Picc.
Ob.
Cl.
Bsn.
Hn.
Tpt.
Timp.
Trgl.
Tamb.
Cym.
B.D.
1
Vn.
2
Va.
Vc./D.B.
67
68
ff
a 2
[tr]

71
Picc.
Ob.
Cl.
Bsn.
Hn.
Tpt.
Trgl.
Tamb.
Cym.
B.D.
1
Vn.
2
Va.
Vc./D.B.
75
76
Picc.
Ob.
Cl.
Bsn.
Hn.
Tpt.
Trgl.
Tamb.
Cym.
B.D.
76
1
Vn.
2
Va.
Vc.
D.B.
p
p
unis.
p
p
p

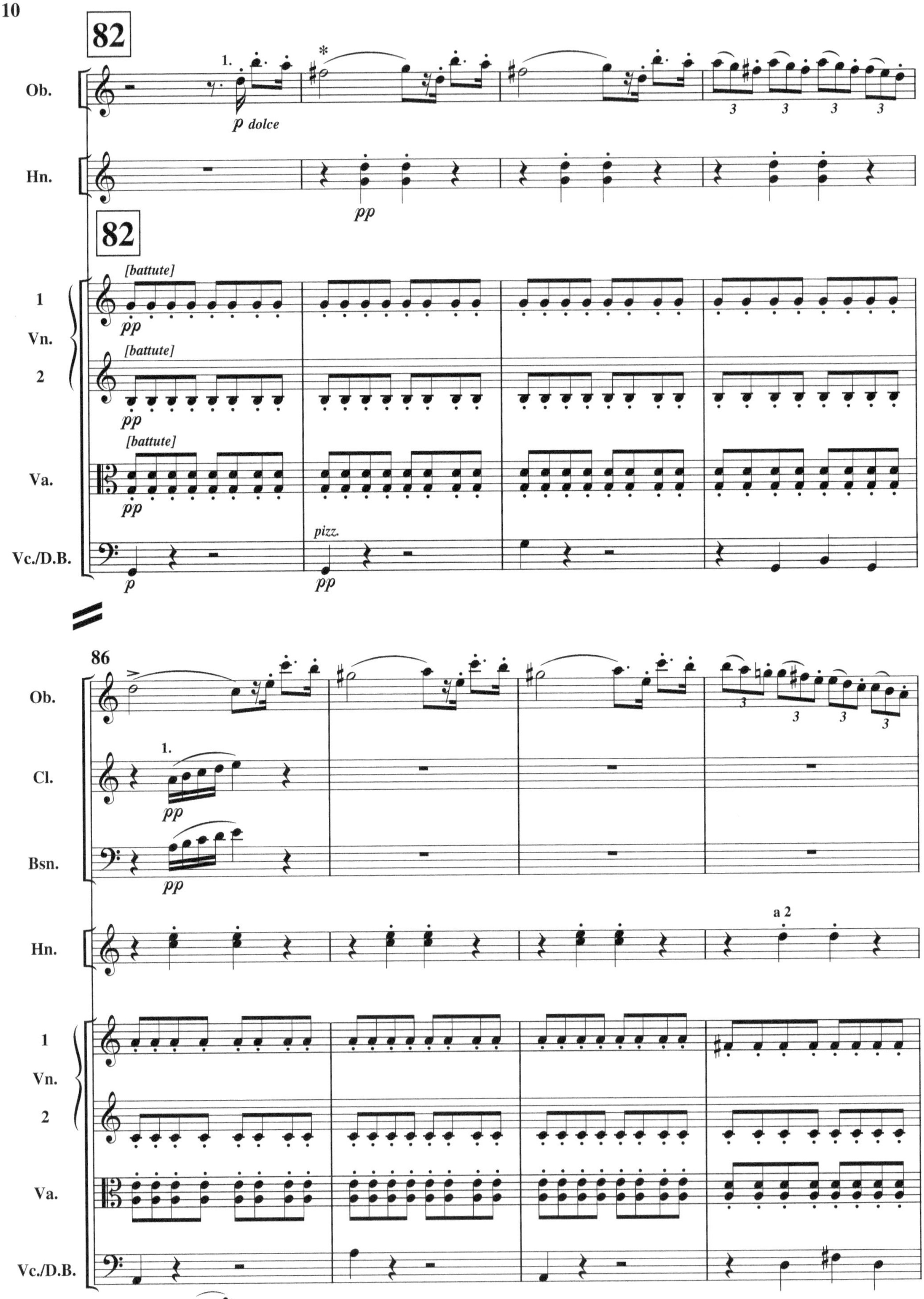

90
Picc.
Ob.
1
Vn.
2
Va.
arco [battute]
Vc./D.B.
p
(pp)
94
Picc.
Ob.
1.
p dolce
Cl.
1.
p dolce
Hn.
pp
1
Vn.
2
Va.
Vc./D.B.
pizz.
pp
3

98
Ob.
Cl.
pp
p
Bsn.
pp
Hn.
a 2
1
Vn.
2
Va.
Vc./D.B.
102
Picc.
p
Ob.
1
Vn.
2
Va.
arco [battute]
Vc./D.B.

106
Picc.
Ob.
1.
p
Hn.
pp
106
[arco]
1
Vn.
2
pp
Va.
pp
Vc./D.B.
pp
110
Picc.
p
Ob.
a 2
Cl.
p
Hn.
p
a 2
1
Vn.
2
p
[arco]
p
[arco]
Va.
p
[arco]
Vc./D.B.
p

14

* No *crescendo* is indicated here, but compare with the corresponding passage beginning in m. 216.
** In some sources, the Bassoon is tacet after the first note of m. 118 until the beginning of m. 122, but it plays throughout the corresponding passage at mm. 220-223.

122
Picc.
Ob.
Cl.
Bsn.
Hn.
Tpt.
a 2
p cresc.
Timp.
Trgl.
Tamb.
Cym.
B.D.
a 2
1
Vn.
2
Va.
Vc.
D.B.
f cresc.

128
126
Picc.
Ob.
Cl.
Bsn.
Hn.
Tpt.
Timp.
Trgl.
Tamb.
Cym.
B.D.
ff
128
posizione normale
1
Vn.
2
posizione normale
Va.
Vc.
D.B.

130
Picc.
Ob.
Cl.
Bsn.
Hn.
Tpt.
a 2
Timp.
Trgl.
Tamb.
Cym.
B.D.
1
Vn.
2
Va.
Vc./D.B.
135
139
a 2
a 2
139
p

140
1
Vn.
2
Va.
Vc.
D.B.
146
Picc.
Ob.
Cl.
Bsn.
Hn.
Tpt.
Timp.
Trgl.
Tamb.
Cym.
B.D.
a 2
146
div.
unis.
p
sf

151
154
Picc.
Ob.
Cl.
Bsn.
Hn.
Tpt.
a 2
Timp.
Trgl.
Tamb.
Cym.
B.D.
154
1
Vn.
2
Va.
div.
unis.
Vc./D.B.
156
Picc.
Ob.
1.
1
Vn.
2
Va.
div.
unis.
Vc./D.B.

161
162
Picc.
Ob.
Cl.
Bsn.
p cresc.
cresc.
p
162
1
Vn.
2
Va.
Vc./D.B.
div.
165
Hn.
Tpt.
Timp.
Trgl.
Tamb.
Cym.
B.D.
a 2
f

169
Picc.
Ob.
Cl.
Bsn.
Hn.
Tpt.
Timp.
Trgl.
Tamb.
Cym.
B.D.
1
Vn.
2
Va.
Vc./D.B.
173
a 2
unis.

177
178
Picc.
Ob.
Cl.
Bsn.
Hn.
Tpt.
Timp.
Trgl.
Tamb.
Cym.
B.D.
178
1
Vn.
2
Va.
Vc.
D.B.
p
184
Picc.
Bsn.
Hn.
pp
184
[battute]
[battute]
[battute]
pizz.
Vc./D.B.

188
Picc.
Ob.
a 2
pp
Bsn.
Hn.
1
Vn.
2
Va.
div.
Vc./D.B.
192
Picc.
Ob.
1.
p
Bsn.
192
1
Vn.
2
Va.
unis.
arco [battute]
Vc./D.B.

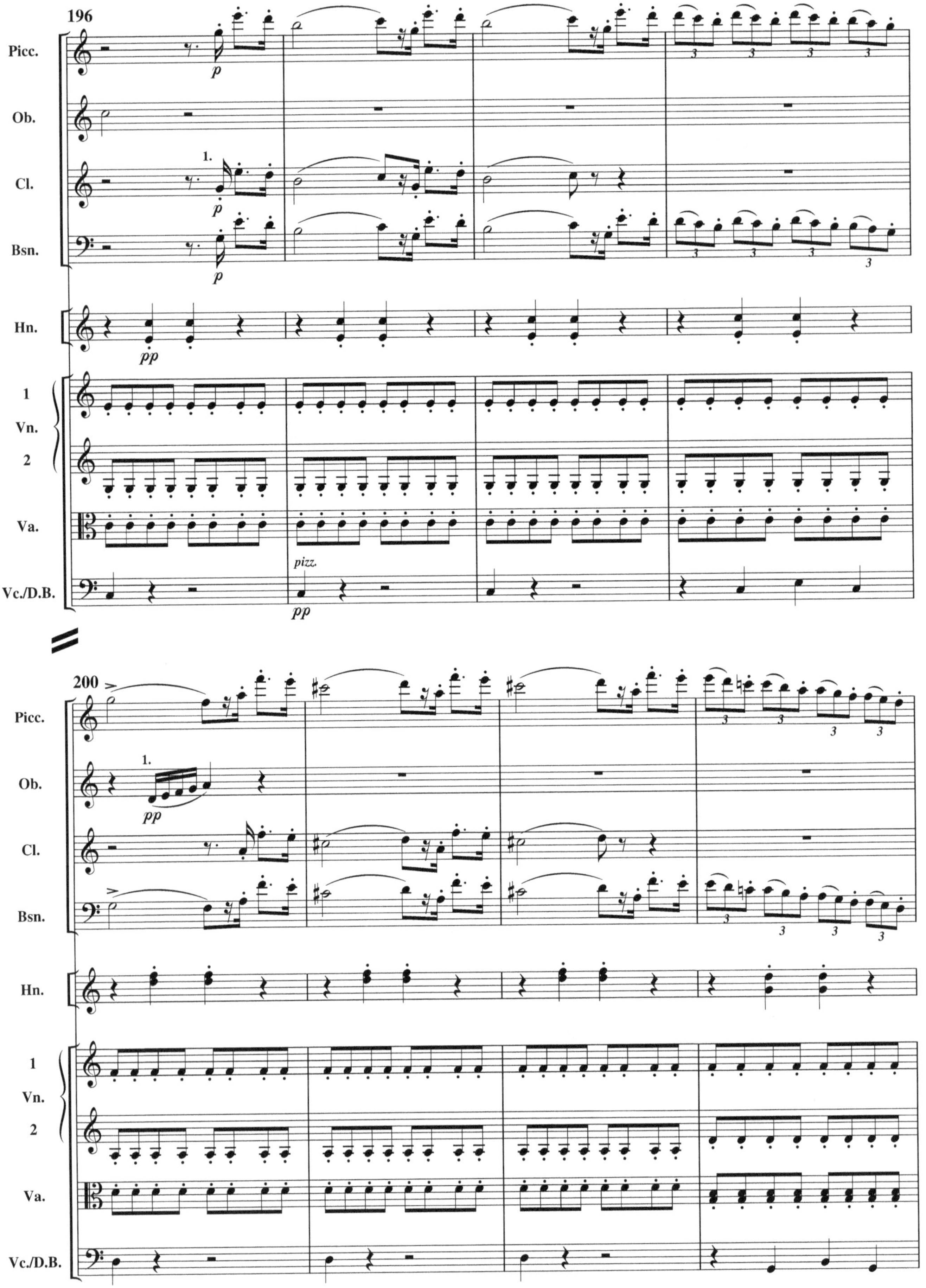
196
Picc.
Ob.
Cl.
Bsn.
Hn.
1
Vn.
2
Va.
Vc./D.B.
p
1.
pp
pizz.
200

204
Picc.
Ob.
Bsn.
1.
p
204
1
Vn.
2
Va.
Vc./D.B.
unis.
arco [battute]
208
Picc.
Ob.
Cl.
Bsn.
p
pp
pp
1
Vn.
2
Va.
Vc./D.B.
[arco]
pp
pp
pp
pp

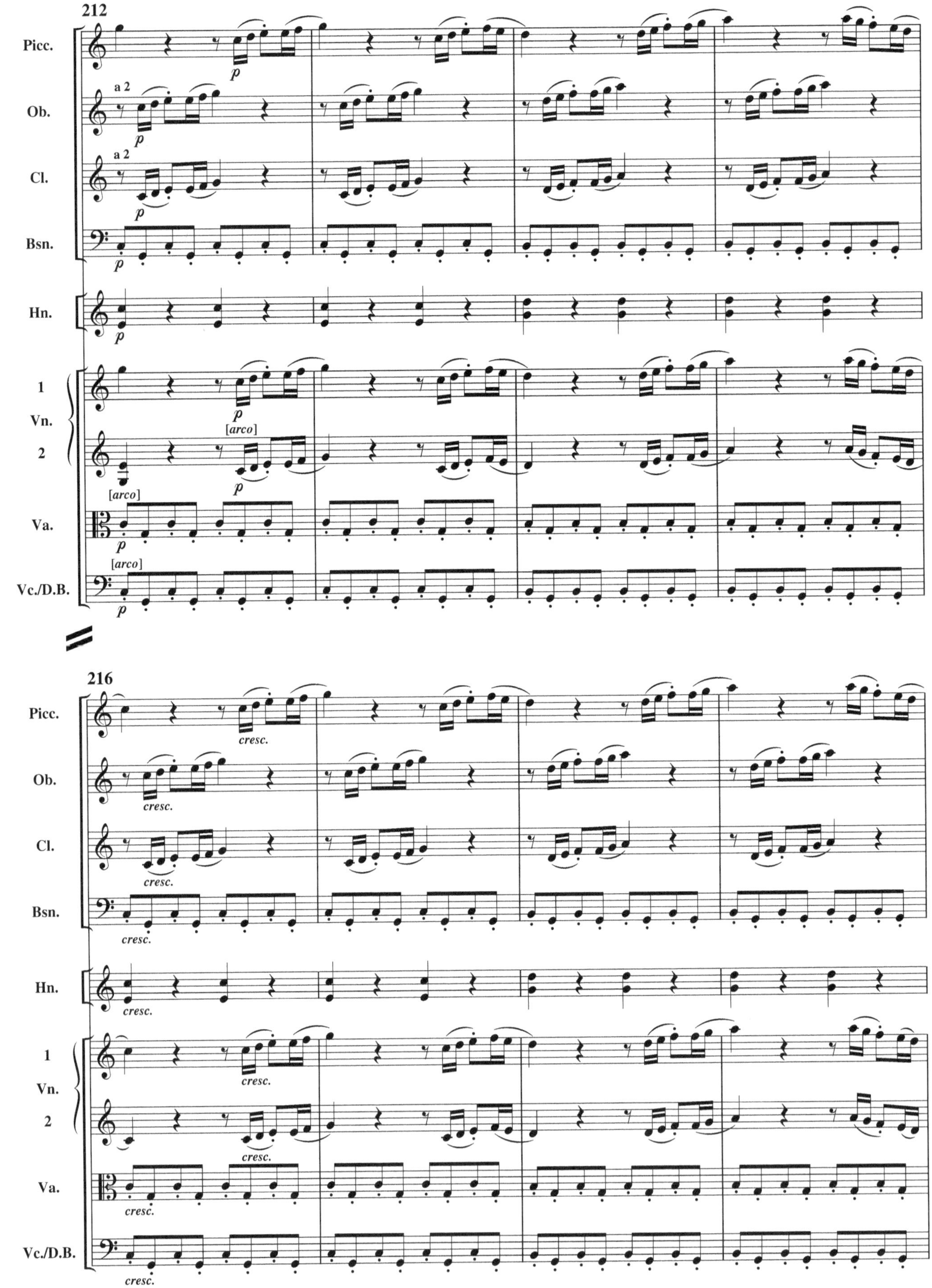
212
Picc.
Ob.
a 2
Cl.
a 2
Bsn.
Hn.
1
Vn.
2
Va.
Vc./D.B.
p
[arco]
216
cresc.

220
Picc.
Ob.
Cl.
Bsn.
Hn.
Tpt.
Trgl.
Tamb.
Cym.
B.D.
a 2
cresc.
p cresc.
220
al ponticello
div.
1
Vn.
2
Va.
Vc./D.B.
225
f cresc.
Timp.
f

230
Picc.
Ob.
Cl.
Bsn.
Hn.
Tpt.
Timp.
Trgl.
Tamb.
Cym.
B.D.
ff
a 2
posizione normale
unis.
1
Vn.
2
Va.
Vc./D.B.
236

241
Picc.
Ob.
a 2
Cl.
Bsn.
Hn.
Tpt.
Timp.
Trgl.
Tamb.
Cym.
B.D.
241
1
Vn.
2
Va.
Vc./D.B.
246

www.ingramcontent.com/pod-product-compliance
Lightning Source LLC
Chambersburg PA
CBHW081155040426
42445CB00015B/1890